THE TRAVELING CONSULTANT'S GUIDE

TO

AUDITING UNIX

First Edition

The Traveling Consultant's Guide to Auditing UNIX

First Edition

Copyright © 2012 by Mark Adams

All rights reserved. No part of this book may be reproduced in any form or by any electronic or mechanical means including information storage and retrieval systems, without permission in writing from the author. The only exception is by a reviewer, who may quote short excerpts in a review.

Printed in the United States of America

First Printing: March, 2012

ISBN-978-1-105-61639-6

Contents

Introduction	XIII
A Word About "Best Practices"	XVIII
Overview	1
General UNIX Auditing	3
Auditing Solaris	20
Auditing Red Hat Enterprise Server	27
Auditing AIX	32
Auditing HP-UX	40
Appendix	51

Introduction

The primary reason for this handbook is that I found that although there are some checklists out there for *auditing* UNIX, they don't really focus on securing the *data*. Checklists are good, but to a point. In many cases, solutions are not nearly as simple as they are made out to be.

When auditing UNIX (and other IT environments), it is important to understand the data flow, including interfaces and access points. Compounding the situation is the fact that there can be many ways to access the data, multiple copies of the data, and data that is transmitted and/or stored *outside* of the database (backup tapes, third party systems, etc.).

From a threat perspective, the insider is widely considered to be the most dangerous, and for obvious reasons. He's already familiar with the environment, probably has a network logon ID, and is "trusted" by his coworkers and management. That's not to say that external threats ("hackers") should be ignored, but it's generally more difficult for such an individual to launch an attack since he must overcome external security mechanisms like the firewalls and intrusion detection/prevention systems (assuming those are in place and are configured appropriately).

The bottom line is this: do not rely too heavily on checklists. Do your research, ask the right questions, and look at what really matters.

A Word About "Best Practices"

There are many "mainstream" security sources that make various (and sometimes conflicting) recommendations regarding UNIX security. It is therefore critical that the auditor gather as much information as possible in order to ensure that all audit findings and recommendations are reasonable and take into account all relevant business and application requirements.

As always, the cost of implementing a recommendation must be balanced against its potential benefit(s).

OVERVIEW

UNIX is not a single operating system. It has many flavors (aka. variants, types, or implementations). Although based on a core set of UNIX commands, different flavors have their own unique commands and features, and are designed to work with different types of hardware. The major ones are listed below.

- Solaris from Sun Microsystems (now owned by Oracle Corp.)

- AIX from IBM*

- HP-UX from HP*

- BSD (Berkeley Software Distribution) UNIX from the University of California at Berkeley

- Linux** from Linus Torvalds

Since there are so many similarities between the various UNIX flavors and distributions, those similarities will be covered first in the General UNIX Auditing section. The sections that follow will focus on the concepts and components that are specific to individual UNIX brands. Those brands include:

- Solaris

- Red Hat Enterprise Linux (RHEL)

- AIX
- HP-UX

* Also sell Linux-based systems
** There are both free and commercial distributions, such as those offered by Red Hat, Inc.

GENERAL UNIX AUDITING

Basic UNIX Permissions

There are three basic permissions:

- (r)ead
- (w)rite
- e(x)ecute.

Permissions are defined for three types of users:

- the owner of the file
- the group that the owner belongs to
- other users

Thus, UNIX file permissions consist of nine bits of information (3 types
 of permissions x 3 type of users), with each having just one of two
values: allowed or denied.

Permissions can be represented textually or numerically.

The table below represents a single octet, meaning that each of the three positions is assigned a value which, when added together, can be anywhere from 0 to 7. The values are:

```
 -  -  -
 4  2  1
```

If the position is occupied then the corresponding value applies. For example, "- - x" equals "1" because the "x" is present and its value is "1". The combination of "r - x" equals "5" because the "r" is present and its value is 4, and together with the "x" (1) adds up to "5".

Note that the "-" symbol replaces "r", "w" or "x" if according access type is denied.

Numeric	Textual
0	---
1	--x
2	-w-
3	-wx
4	r--
5	r-x
6	rw-
7	rwx

Permissions in directory listings consist of ten characters.

```
 -  rwx  r--  r--
 0  123  456  789
```

The symbol in position 0 ("-") denotes the type of the file. It is either "d" if the item is a directory, "l" if it is a link, or "-" if the item is a regular file.

Symbols in positions 1 to 3 ("rwx") are permissions for the **owner** of the file.
Symbols in positions 4 to 6 ("r--") are permissions for the **group**.
Symbols in positions 7 to 9 ("r--") are permissions for **others** (everyone else).

Differences in Access

Access Type	File	Folder
Read	File contents can be read	The directory listing can be obtained
Write	User or process can write to the file (change its contents)	User or process can change directory contents somehow: create new or delete existing files in the directory or

5

		rename files.
Execute	File can be executed	User or process can access the directory; that is, go to it (make it to be the current working directory)

Umask

Each user's umask specifies modes that are NOT to be set on new files and directories. Common values are 022, 027, and 077.

The default system umask is usually 022 (use the umask command to show it).

For maximum safety, the value should be 027, or 077.

Umask Example:

```
666 Base permissions of test.doc  (rw-rw-rw-)
022 umask value ("Do NOT set the 'w' permission")
---- subtract
644 permissions of new file (rw-r--r--)
```

Web Server Permissions

The web server assigns the rights of the web-server-specific user, typically user "nobody", to the connected web client, as if "nobody" is connected to the web server.

"Nobody" belongs to the "other" group, and thus it inherits permissions that "others" have to the files.

Generic files such as html or images usually need to have 644 permissions so that the "nobody" user can read them.

Scripts usually need 755 rights so that "nobody" can read and execute them (but not write to them).

Other Bits

In addition to the basic permissions discussed earlier, there are three bits of information defined for files in UNIX:

- SUID or setuid: change user ID on execution. If the setuid bit is set, then when the file is executed by a user, the process will have the same rights as the owner of the file being executed.

- SGID or setgid: change group ID on execution. Same as above, but inherits rights of the group of the owner of the file.

- Sticky bit. In the past it was used to trigger a process to "stick" in memory after it finished, but now this usage is obsolete.

Examples of SUID and SGID:

- SUID

- If set, it replaces the "x" in the owner permissions to "s", if owner has execute permissions, or to "S" otherwise.

    -rws------ both owner execute and SUID are set

    -r-S------ SUID is set, but owner execute is not set

- SGID

    - If set, it replaces "x" in the group permissions to "s", if group has execute permissions, or to "S" otherwise.

    -rwxrws--- both group execute and SGID are set

    -rwxr-S--- SGID is set, but group execute is not set

Finding "Risky" Files

SUID and SGID files can pose a significant security risk, so it is important to include them in a UNIX audit. The following commands can be used to search for them.

find / \(-perm -4000 -o -perm -2000 \) -type f -exec ls -ldb {} \;

OR

find / -type f -perm +6000 –ls

In addition, files and directories that are writable by everyone ("world writable") should be listed as well since they can pose a huge risk. To do this, have the administrator run the following commands:

Find all world writable directories:

find / -perm -0002 -type d –print

Find all world writable files:

find / -perm -0002 -type f –print

find / -perm -2 ! -type l -ls

Recommended Practices

- Never make setuid shell scripts.

- All setuid to root programs should be in system directories and not readable or writable by "other".

- Any "setuid-to-user" program should be known to the user.

- Ensure that only 'root' has a UID of '0' (zero).

Passwords

UNIX passwords allow mixed case, numbers, and symbols. Typically the maximum password length on a standard UNIX system is 8 characters, although some systems (or system enhancements) allow up to 16 characters.

If shadow passwords are not in use, password hashes will be located in the /etc/passwd file, which is very insecure since this file must allow read access to everyone.

Passwords can be fed into a password cracker like John the Ripper to be tested for strength. If shadow passwords are being used then you need to obtain both the **/etc/passwd** and **/etc/shadow** files to do this (root access will be required to obtain the /etc/shadow files). John the Ripper is a free, open source program that can be downloaded from http://www.openwall.com/john/.

The shadow file contains the encrypted form of the password (the "hash"). It should only be readable by root! The location of this file depends on the UNIX flavor:

- AIX /etc/security/passwd
- HP-UX 9.x /.secure/etc/passwd
- HP-UX 10.x /tcb/files/auth
- HP-UX 11i v1.6 /etc/shadow
- Solaris /etc/shadow
- Linux /etc/shadow

Startup Files

Examine start up files. The following shows where startup files are typically located based on the UNIX flavor.

```
AIX              /etc/rc
BDS              /etc/rc
Linux (Red Hat)  /etc/rc.d/rc
Solaris          /etc/rc*.d (where "*" is a number)
```

Network Security

The **.rhosts** file resides in the user's home directory (denoted by "$HOME").
It specifies all the host names of the remote UNIX machines that the user can log into without a password (using the same username and password as those for his current machine). If used, permissions on the file should be 600 (rw- --- ---).

The **/etc/hosts.equiv**, **/etc/hosts.allow**, **/etc/hosts.deny** files specify the remote hosts (or allowed or denied) that can log on to the current computer without the remote user having to provide a password.

The **$HOME/.netrc** file may be created by any user in his or her home directory. This file allows certain users to connect to the host with ftp or rexec without supplying a password.

These files pose a significant security risk and should be reviewed for appropriateness!

Inetd.conf

The **/etc/inetd.conf** file is the default configuration file for the **inetd** daemon* (pronounced "demon"), and it specifies which daemons start by default. An example snippet is below:

```
#ftp    stream tcp nowait root /usr/sbin/tcpd  wu.ftpd
#telnet stream tcp nowait root /usr/sbin/tcpd  in.telnetd
node    stream tcp nowait root /usr/sbin/node  node
listen  stream tcp nowait root /usr/bin/listen listen -a -c -r -t
```

```
#finger stream tcp nowait root /usr/sbin/tcpd in.fingerd
#login stream tcp nowait root /usr/etc/rlogind rlogind
uucp stream tcp nowait /etc/uucpd uucpd
exec stream tcp nowait /etc/rexecd rexecd
ssh stream tcp nowait root /usr/sbin/sshd sshd -i
```

A "#" sign indicates that the line is commented out and will therefore not be executed.

* UNIX daemons are like services in Windows

Auditing inetd.conf

- Ensure that insecure daemons are disabled.* These include:
    - Rexecd
    - Rlogind
    - Rshd (server for both **rsh** and **rcp** commands)
    - Tftpd
    - Fingerd
    - Telnetd
    - IP small services (echo, daytime, qotd, chargen, and discard)
    - Check to see if Secure Shell (SSH) is being used instead of Telnet. For a detailed explanation of SSH see the Appendix.

* Also check the */etc/pam.conf* file to make sure that entries for the "r*" services (rlogin, rexec, etc.) are commented out.

Controlling Root Access

In many cases it may be desirable to put additional controls on 'root' access. There are several ways to do this:

- The **wheel** group is a group which limits the number of people who are able to 'su' (switch user) to root. This usually consists of a group named "wheel" and a set of users that are permitted to use the utility 'su' in order to change to root.

- An empty **/etc/securetty** file prevents root login on any devices attached to the computer. Note also that attempts to log in as root will be logged.

- Edit the /etc/passwd file and change the shell from /bin/bash to /sbin/nologin.

- Edit the /etc/ssh/sshd_config file and set the PermitRootLogin parameter to 'no'.

Scheduler (Cron)

Cron is the name of program that enables UNIX users to execute commands or scripts automatically at a specified time/date.

Cron runs as a daemon called *crond*. Crontab (CRON TABle) is a file which contains the schedule of cron entries to be run and at specified times.

Example: this line in a crontab file removes the tmp files from
/home/someuser/tmp each day at 6:30 PM.
     30 18 * * *   rm /home/someuser/tmp/*

- The first field is minutes (0-59)

- The second field is the hours (0-23)
- The third field reflects the day of the month (0-31)
- The fourth field reflects the month of the year (1-12)
- The fifth field reflects the day of the week (0-6 with Sunday = 0)
- The last field reflects the process to run
- The * means every occurrence of the field

The use of cron can be restricted through the /usr/lib/cron.allow and /usr/lib/cron.deny files.

If only cron.deny exists and is empty, all users can use crontab. If neither file exists, only the root user can use crontab.

Audit the programs that are scheduled to execute for appropriateness. Jobs
are usually located in /var/spool/cron/crontabs and/or /usr/spool/cron/crontabs . Also, check the file permissions on the crontab itself.

The most critical crontab entry will be the root owned crontab. Permissions should be 600 (rw- --- ---).

NFS

Network File System, or NFS, allows a system to share directories and files with others over a network (similar to Windows file sharing). There are usually three daemons that must be running on the NFS server:

nfsd	Services requests from the NFS clients
mountd	Carries out the requests that nfsd passes on to it
rpcbind	Allows NFS clients to discover which port the NFS server is using

The **/etc/exports** file specifies which file systems NFS should export (or "share"), as well as access options.

Examples: /Data   host1.mydomain.com(ro,root_squash)
            /Home   host1.mydomain.com(rw,john_doe)

"ro" means read-only; "rw" means read-write

"root_squash" prevents write access for root

To find NFS mounts use the 'showmount' command to display the exports of a given host:

/usr/etc/showmount -e hostname

Tip:
There is a little-known free package from Microsoft called Services for UNIX (SFU) which allows Windows users to run UNIX commands like **showmount** from within a Windows command prompt.

Auditing NFS

- Understand that NFS is inherently insecure!

- Confirm that the latest patches have been applied.

- Audit all exported file systems for appropriateness (i.e. there should be no unnecessary exports).

- Ensure that no file systems are exported to the world or to untrusted hosts.

- If an NFS share is exported as read-only, consider using the **all_squash** option, which makes every user accessing the exported file system take the userid of the *nobody* user on the server.

- Wildcards should be used sparingly when exporting NFS shares as the scope of the wildcard may encompass more systems than intended.

NIS

Network Information Service, formerly known as the Yellow Pages, is a distributed database system that centralizes commonly accessed UNIX files like /etc/passwd, /etc/group, or /etc/hosts.

The information accessed in NIS is housed in files called maps. In addition to the central master server, where all maps are maintained, and the clients that access them, slave servers exist.

ANY user who knows the NIS domain name can access the NIS server and obtain the maps!

Auditing NIS

- Understand that NIS is inherently insecure!
- Confirm that the latest patches have been applied.

- Ensure that on the master NIS server, the server's password file and the NIS password file are separate so that all users in the NIS password file do not automatically gain access to the NIS master server.

- Check to see if the "securenets" feature is being used. Securenets can restrict access to a given set of hosts. This file is typically found in **/var/yp/securenets**.

- Ensure that shadow passwords are being used.

X-Windows

X-Windows (X11) allows applications to connect to the user interface on the same computer system, or on another system located elsewhere on the network. Using this capability, users can log in to a remote machine and run applications that open windows and interact with the user at his or her desktop.

Security is minimal, so other means must be used to secure X11 connections. The best, and most recommended, strategy is to use X11 forwarding over SSH for secure remote X connections.

The SSH server configuration file (e.g. /etc/ssh2/sshd2_config) should contain:

>   AllowX11Forwarding yes

The SSH server configuration file should contain:

>   ForwardX11   yes

Finally, just having X-Windows running on a UNIX server should be questioned since it is normally unnecessary.

Sudo

Sudo (superuser do) is a freely available package that allows a system administrator to give certain users (or groups of users) the ability to run some (or all) commands as root or another user, while logging the commands and arguments that are entered.
Activities are logged to the *sulog* file:

- Solaris, AIX and HP-UX: **/var/adm/sulog**

- Linux: **/var/log/secure** and/or **/var/adm/messages**

The **/etc/sudoers** file contains a list of which users may execute which programs.

Restricted Shells

Restricted shells are used to limit the operations allowed for particular user accounts. They prevent users from:

- Changing directories
- Setting the $PATH variable
- Specifying path or command names beginning with "/"
- Redirecting output

Some of the major shells that can be used are: sh, csh, bash, ksh

Check for entries similar to the following in the user's login script:

```
#!/bin/sh
exec /bin/bash -r
```

AUDITING SOLARIS

Solaris Hardening

"Hardening" refers to the implementation of controls to strengthen the security of an operating system. For Solaris, use the Solaris Security Tookit to harden and audit the OS.

Formerly known as the JumpStart Architecture and Security Scripts (JASS) toolkit, it supports Solaris 8, 9 and 10.

Also, look for the following lines in the /etc/system file to prevent buffer overflow attacks:

>   set noexec_user_stack=1
>   set noexec_user_stack_log=1

PFEXEC

The Solaris **pfexec** command functions as a passwordless 'su' or 'sudo' in Linux and other UNIX flavors.

Implemented by assigning regular users to the "Primary Administrator" profile in the **/etc/security/exec_attr** file.

Users with this profile simply type "pfexec" and then the desired command, without having to log in as root or supply the root password.

Check the **/etc/security/user_attr** file to see who has this profile.

Password Policy

Examine **/etc/default/passwd** for password settings. You can even define a dictionary file to check new passwords against.

An example is below:

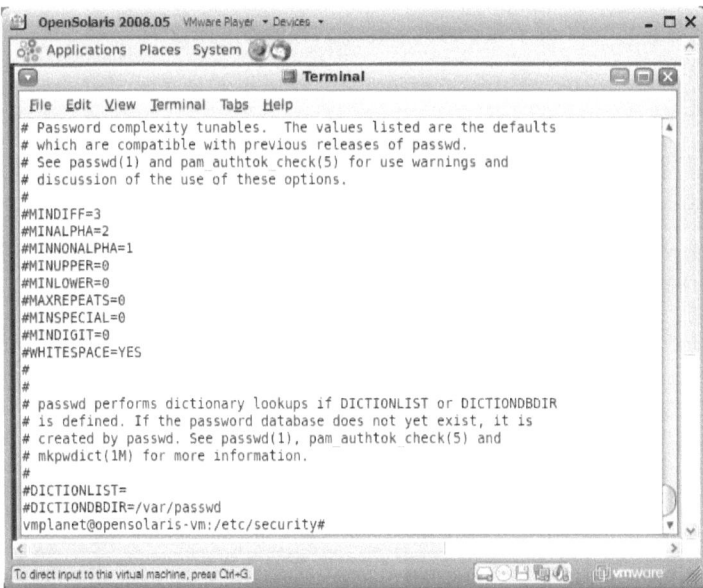

NFS and SMB Shares

The 'sharemgr' command is used to manage NFS shares:

- **sharemgr list –v** (view share group's properties)
- **sharemgr show –v** (view shares)
- **sharemgr show –vp** (view share properties)

For SMB (Windows) shares:

- SMB functionality does not ship with Solaris 10, but it can be added (it's free).
- Check **/etc/sfw/smb.conf**

Solaris Audit Features

- The audit daemon uses six files located in **/etc/security**

- The **/etc/security/audit_startup** script contains the audit settings

- The **/etc/security/audit_event** file contains the events to be audited

- Audit records are normally written to the **/var/audit** directory, but they could be elsewhere (check the **/etc/security/audit_control** file for location)

- Permissions on this file should be 750 (rwx r-x ---)

- The **/etc/security/audit_event** file contains the events to be audited.

- The **/etc/security/audit_class** file contains the classes of events.

- Use the following command to see if the audit daemon is running:
    # svcs | grep "auditd"

- Custom auditing can be configured on a per user basis.
    - Check the **audit_control** and **audit_user** files

- The **auditconfig** command provides a command line interface to get and set audit configuration information and audit policy.

- The **praudit** command makes the records readable.

- The **auditreduce** command enables selecting particular audit records and merging the records into one audit trail.

Log files can be found in the following locations:

- /var/adm/sulog – logs all 'su' attempts
- /var/adm/messages

- /var/log/syslog – controlled by /etc/syslog.conf
    - By default, AUTH messages don't get logged to any logfiles, so check the syslog.conf to make sure it is configured to do this!
    - http://www.softpanorama.org/Logs/syslog.shtml
    - /var/log/authlog (or /var/adm/authlog)
- /var/adm/utmpx (must use 'w', 'who', or 'users')
- /var/adm/wtmpx (must use 'last')

Solaris Zones

Zones act as completely isolated virtual servers within a single operating system instance.

- Initial default zone is the Global Zone
- Zones operate with fewer privileges than their global zone counterpart.

Processes that are running in one zone cannot monitor or affect processes that are running in other zones (including those running with superuser credentials!)

When auditing zones, look in the **/etc/security/audit_startup** file for the following line:

    /usr/sbin/auditconfig -setpolicy +zonename

Because each zone can be configured differently with regard to auditing users, it is possible for the *audit_user* file to be empty.

RBAC

Solaris allows administrators to define roles, give them privileges and assign users to those roles. This is referred to as Role-Based Access Control (RBAC).

The RBAC system stores the role assignments in the /etc/user_attr file. Roles, like user accounts, can be assigned passwords.

For more information on RBAC visit Sun's web site below:

http://docs.sun.com/app/docs/doc/816-4557/prbactm-1?a=view

The following files and directories are used is auditing RBAC:

- **/etc/user_attr**
    - Defines extended user attributes

- **/etc/security/auth_attr**
    - Defines authorizations

- **/etc/security/prof_attr**
    - Defines profiles (there are 70 predefined profiles)

- **/etc/security/policy.conf**

- Defines policy for the system

Can also view profiles by clicking on System → Administration → User and Groups

AUDITING RED HAT ENTERPRISE LINUX

"General UNIX Auditing" material applies to RHEL, with a few twists:

- There is no **/var/adm** directory in RHEL.
- Check **/etc/login.defs** for account and password restrictions.

SELinux

Security Enhanced Linux was developed by the NSA in 2001. It is not a distribution, but rather a set of modifications that can be applied to a UNIX-like OS. It implements mandatory access control (MAC) and role-based access control (RBAC).

SELinux RBAC provides the following features:

- Determines which roles users can adopt and what they can do.

- Works along with Type Enforcement.

- Users are assigned roles by user statement.

-ex: **user john roles { staff_r sysadm_r};**

- Transitions between roles are governed by allow statement.
    - ex: **allow staff_r sysadm_r;**

- Roles are authorized to enter domains by the role statement.
    - ex: **role sysadm_r types ifconfig_t**

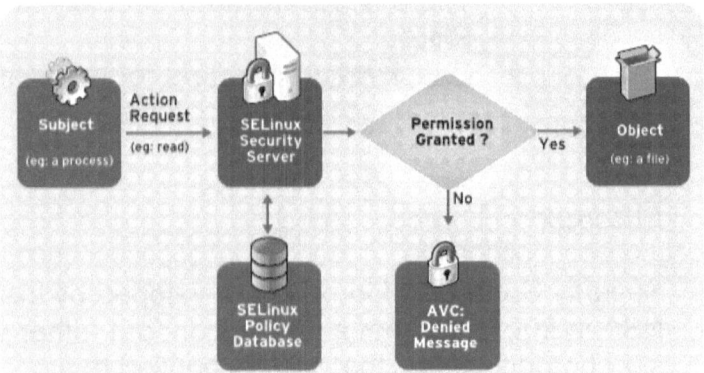

Image from redhat.com

Auditing and Logging

Log files are saved in the **/var/log/audit/audit.log** file.

The **/etc/auditd.conf**, **/etc/audit.rules**, and **/etc/sysconfig/auditd** files control the audit configuration.

The **/etc/rc.d/init.d/auditd** script controls the audit subsystem

The Audit package includes six files located in the /sbin directory:

- **autrace** – trace a specific process
- **ausearch** – query audit logs
- **auditctl** – controls behavior of the *auditd* server
- **auditd** – the audit daemon
- **aureport** – produces summary reports
- **audispd** – relays events to remote machines or analyzes events for suspicious behavior

There is also a set of auditing rules that can be defined and applied. There are three lists: task, entry and exit

There are also three actions: never, always and possible
This example checks all files opened by the user with the uid of 501:

    -a exit,always –S open –F loginuid=501

See the **auditctl** manual page for more information.

Two other Linux security packages worth noting are **AppArmor** and **grsecurity**.

AppArmor (Application Armor) is maintained and released by Novell. It was created as an alternative to SELinux. It's biggest advantage over SELinux is that its policies and tools are easier to understand. However it only runs on the Suse and Opensuse Linux distributions.

grsecurity is a set of patches for the Linux kernel with an emphasis on enhancing security. It utilizes a multi-layered detection, prevention, and containment model. Its main advantage is ease of use for users new to Linux security, plus it will run on any Linux distribution.

Other Security Features

Most Linux distributions support the ability to block and log port scans. A port scanner (such as nmap) is a piece of software designed to search a network host for open ports. Crackers can use nmap to scan your network before starting attack. A program called **psad** (port scan attack detector) is commonly used to address such attacks.

The default psad file is located at /etc/psad/psad.conf. To view a psad scan report simply type:

```
# psad -S
```

There are also several intrusion detection software packages available for the Linux platform. The two most popular are Snort and OSSEC.

RHEL 4 and 5 Resources

- Red Hat Enterprise Linux 5.2 – Deployment Guide

http://www.centos.org/docs/5/html/5.2/Deployment_Guide/

- Red Hat Enterprise Linux 4: Red Hat SELinux Guide

 http://www.linuxtopia.org/online_books/centos_linux_guides/centos_selinux_guide/

- Red Hat Enterprise Linux Documentation

 http://www.redhat.com/docs/manuals/enterprise/#RHEL5

AUDITING AIX

Key Permissions

Verify that the permissions for the following files are set correctly:

-rw-rw-r--	root system	/etc/filesystems
-rw-rw-r--	root system	/etc/hosts
-rw-------	root system	/etc/inittab
-rw-r--r--	root system	/etc/vfs
-rw-r--r--	root system	/etc/security/failedlogin
-rw-rw----	root audit	/etc/security/audit/hosts

Network Services

- Use securetcpip command to enhance network security

- Disables the following:
    - Rcp
    - Rlogin and Rlogind
    - Rsh and Rshd
    - Tftp and Tftpd
    - Evidence this by checking the /etc/security/config file and looking for this stanza:

    tcpip:
    netrc = ftp,rexec   /*
functions disabling netrc */

Key Files and Directories

/etc/group - Contains the basic group attributes.

/etc/passwd - Contains the basic user attributes.

/etc/security/audit/config Contains audit system configuration information.

/etc/security/environ Contains the environment attributes of users.

/etc/security/group Contains the extended attributes of groups.

/etc/security/limits Contains the process resource limits of users.

/etc/security/login.cfg Contains configuration information for user log in and authentication.

/etc/security/passwd Contains password information.

/usr/lib/security/mkuser.default Contains default user configurations.

/etc/security/user Contains extended user attributes.

/etc/security/lastlog Contains last login information.

/etc/inetd.conf, **/etc/inittab**, **/etc/rc.nfs**, and **/etc/rc.tcpip** Contain daemon and service information.

AIX Trusted System

The Trusted Computing Base (TCB) provides very useful tools for both security and system integrity.

Use the **syschk.cfg** file and the **tcbck** command to verify that attributes in various files are correct.

Other TCB "check" commands that are useful are:

> **usrck** verifies that all users listed as group members in a group are defined as users on the system, that the GID is unique in the system, and that the group name is correctly formed.
>
> **grpck** verifies parameters of a UID and also looks for duplicate UIDs.
>
> **pwdck** checks authorization stanzas in **/etc/passwd** and **/etc/security/passwd**.

AIX Security Expert

AIX Security Expert is a native tool for configuring and hardening the system. Per the AIX Security Expert web page,

> "AIX Security Expert provides simple menu settings for High Level Security,

Medium Level Security, Low Level Security, and AIX Standard Settings security that integrate over 300 security configuration settings while still providing control over each security element for advanced administrators. AIX Security Expert can be used to implement the appropriate level of security, without the necessity of reading a large number of papers on security hardening and then individually implementing each security element."

- Three security templates: High, Medium and Low

- There is a **Check Security** option that writes the settings, and any changes, to the file **/etc/security/aixpert/check_report.txt**

- The **Enable binaudit** action button sets audit policy

  - The **/etc/security/audit/config** file must be configured appropriately

  - Audit settings vary by security template

Example: AIX Security Expert

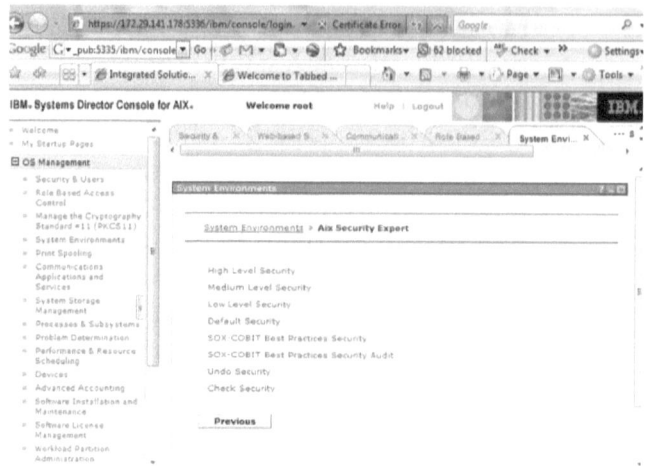

AIX Passwords

- The password policy file is /etc/security/user

- A variety of options can be set, such as:
    - Mindiff
    - Minage (in weeks)
    - Maxage (in weeks)
    - Minlen
    - Minalpha
    - Histsize
    - Maxrepeats
    - Minother

AIX RBAC

Starting with AIX release version 6, the role-based access mechanism is been enhanced.

- **root** access can be disabled.

- **root** tasks are assigned to three system-defined users.

- Privileges, authorization, and roles are assigned as per the users' responsibility.

There are three pre-defined roles assigned to three pre-defined users:

- **ISSO**, the Information System Security Officer

- **SO**, the System Operator

- **SA**, the Security Administrator

User	Role	Responsibilities
ISSO	ISSO	- Establish and maintain security policy - Set passwords for users - Network configuration - Device configuration

SO	SO	- System shutdown reboot - File system backup, restore, and quotas - System error logging, trace, and statistics - Workload administration
SA	SA	- User administration excluding password - Filesystem administration - Software Installation and Update - Network Daemon management and device allocation

Auditing AIX RBAC

The AIX System Management Interface Tool (**SMIT**) provides a menu-based alternative to the command line for managing and maintaining the operating system. It can be used to show users, roles and privileges.

You can also check the /etc/security/user.roles file. Here is an example:

**jdoe:
roles = ManageAllPswds**

Focus on the **ManageAllUsers** and **ManageAllPswds** roles since members of these roles could cause considerable mischief if they wanted to.

AIX Resources

http://www.securitydocs.com/library/3136/2

http://publib.boulder.ibm.com/infocenter/systems/index.jsp?topic=/com.ibm.aix.security/doc/security/aix_sec_expert_remov_unnec_services.htm

http://www.redbooks.ibm.com/abstracts/sg247430.html

http://publib.boulder.ibm.com/infocenter/pseries/v5r3/index.jsp?topic=/com.ibm.aix.security/doc/security/aix_sec_expert.htm

Auditing HP-UX

HP-UX Trusted System

- Auditing must be turned on for normal system operation! Note also that auditng is *not* available on non-trusted systems (known as "standard mode" systems).

- The existence of the file **/tcb/files/auth/system/default** indicates a trusted system.

- Invoke the SAM (System Administration Manager) and select "Auditing and Security" to view the trusted system settings.

- By default, the audit status for all users is set to 'y'.

- New users added to the system are automatically audited.

- All users on the system are required to use passwords.

- An audit ID number is created for each user.

- The audit flag is set for all existing users.

- *at*, *batch* and *crontab* files are converted to use the audit ID of whoever submits them.

- The following are default values for audit monitor and log parameters:

    - Primary log file path name = /.secure/etc/audfile1
    - Primary log file file switch size (AFS) = 1,000KB
    - Auxiliary log file path name = /.secure/etc/audfile2
    - Auxiliary log file switch size (AFS) = 1,000KB
    - Allowable free space minimum (FSS) = 20% of file system
    - Warning messages sent when log reaches 90%

Password Policy

- The password policy is the /etc/default/security file.

- The options below are available on HP-UX 11i:

    PASSWORD_HISTORY_DEPTH=5
    SU_ROOT_GROUP=ADMIN
    ABORT_LOGIN_ON_MISSING_HOMEDIR=1
    MIN_PASSWORD_LENGTH=8
    PASSWORD_MIN_UPPER_CASE_CHARS=2
    PASSWORD_MIN_LOWER_CASE_CHARS=2
    PASSWORD_MIN_DIGIT_CHARS=2
    PASSWORD_MIN_SPECIAL_CHARS=1

```
UMASK=022
PASSWORD_MAXDAYS=60
PASSWORD_MINDAYS=5
PASSWORD_WARNDAYS=7
```

- On trusted systems, the "Use Restriction Rules" option can be used to include a dictionary check.

HP-UX Key Files and Directories

- /etc/inittab
    - Contains startup routines
    - /etc/syslog.conf
    - Specifies rules for system logging
    - /etc/rc.config.d/auditing
    - contains the parameters which control auditing

- /var/adm/cron/log
    - Default log file for cron activities
    - /tcb/files/auth/*/*
    - Used for managing passwords and system access
    - /tcb/files/ttys
    - Terminal login information

Event Categories

The following events can be recorded in the log files:

- Changes to the TCB (attempts to change the kernel or critical databases)

- User authentication (someone attempting to authenticate)

- Configuration changes (changing the system INIT level)

- Initialization of the system (installing new executable programs)

- Data transfer (obtaining or granting privileges and permissions)

- Access to data (reading or modifying data to which the user has no access to)

Security Containment

Introduced in HP-UX 11i v2, Security Containment is built around three core technologies: compartments, fine-grained privileges, and role-based access control (RBAC).

In addition, it makes several trusted mode security features available on standard mode HP-UX systems. These features are called the HP-UX Standard Mode Security Extensions. The HP-UX Standard Mode Security Extensions (SMSE) includes Audit, User Security Database, and Per-User Security Attributes.

Auditing HP-UX RBAC

The HP System Management Homepage (SMH), allows for the management of local RBAC roles, authorizations, and commands through the web interface of SMH Version 2.2 and higher.

You can also examine the contents of the **/etc/rbac** folder and subfolders, specifically the following:

/etc/rbac/user_role   User roles
/etc/rbac/role_auth   Role authorizations
/etc/rbac/cmd_priv   Commands and privileges for each role

HP-UX 11i – Checking Patches

Use SWA (Software Assistant)

- Supersedes the now obsolete Security Patch Check (SPC) tool

- Can perform a variety of checks:

  - published security issues
  - installed patches with warnings
  - missing patches with critical fixes

Can produce reports in HTML format

HP-UX Bastille

HP-UX Bastille is a security hardening and lockdown tool that is similar to AIX Security Expert.

- Generates security-configuration status reports.

    # bastille –assess

- Creates HP-UX Bastille-configuration baselines and compares the current state of the system to the saved baseline (drift).

    # bastille_drift -- from_baseline *baseline*

Trusted System vs. Bastille

Bastille is a completely locked down version of HP-UX. The best use of Bastille" servers are as servers at the edge of the corporate network, like mail relays or web servers, which are directly facing Internet.

Trusted computing is a way of enabling more security features on the HP-UX server, making it easier to audit. This makes the Trusted System a better choice for internal servers.

HP-UX Host Intrusion Detection System

HP-UX 11i v1, v2 and v3 all come with a Host Intrusion Detection System (HIDS). Intrusion detection detects illegal and improper use of computing resources by unauthorized people, before such misuse results in excessive damage. This detection system constantly monitors critical systems and data to protect them from attacks.

The HIDS agent configuration file is called ids.cf, and is located in /etc/opt/ids. The configuration file has five sections:

1. Global Configuration: Parameters that define the overall product structure. Thelogging and interface parameters may be edited by the administrator.

2. Correlator Configuration: Parameters related to the correlator. A parameter canbe configured to take measurements of the system call event rate.

3. Data Source Process (DSP) Configuration: A section per-DSP that defines thesystem files to monitor and level of kernel blocking.

4. Pattern Mapping Section: The HP-UX HIDS detection templates.

5. Remote Communication Section: Parameters required for network communications.

Responses to intrusions can fall into the following four methods:

Forwarding Information
Information about the alert can be forwarded by sending an email or calling a pager. Filtering is required to prevent repeated alerts from causing a storm of pages.

Halting Further Attacks
Automated response can halt further attacks by changing an attribute of the system. For example, disabling an account, disabling remote logins, or changing a directory's access permissions.

Preservation of Evidence
If evidence is to be preserved and analyzed, a response script can halt all further processing on the system. Alternatively, it can disable network connections so that the system is preserved in a running state.

System Restoration to a Stable State
If business continuity is important, the system must be restored to a stable state. If critical files are

modified, they can be restored from trusted read-only media.

The following are global configuration variables:

IDS_ALERTFILE
/var/opt/ids/alert.log
Any alerts resulting from intrusive activity detected by the agent software will be logged to this file.

IDS_ERRORFILE
/var/opt/ids/error.log
Any errors generated in the operation of the agent software will be logged to this file.

IDS_LISTEN_IFACE
""

The IP address or host name associated with the agent system's network interface card.

IDS_RT_RESPONSE_DIR
/opt/ids/rt_response
The automated response directory, containing executable binary or script programs that are executed on the agent node. These programs are executed when a real-time alert is generated and when both the Alert Aggregation and the Real Time Alerts options are enabled. The programs can take any actions that the security administrator deems appropriate.

IDS_RESPONSE_DIR
/opt/ids/response
The automated response directory containing executable binary or script programs that are executed on the agent node. These programs are executed either when alert aggregation is disabled and any alert is generated, or when alert aggregation is enabled and an aggregated alert or an alert that is not or cannot be aggregated is generated. The programs can take any actions that the security administrator deems appropriate.

The following security checks MUST be passed in order for response programs to be run:

- The response directory must not be world-writable, that is, not writable by others.
- The directory must be owned by user *ids*.
- The directory must be local; it cannot be a symbolic link, a pipe, NFS-mounted, and so on.

For a response program to be run:

- A file in the response directory MUST be a local regular file; it cannot be a symbolic link, a pipe, NFS-mounted, and so on.

- A file in the response directory must *not* be world-writable.

HP-UX Resources

- HP-UX System Administrator's Guide: Security Management

  http://docs.hp.com/en/5992-3387/5992-3387.pdf

- HP-UX Standard Mode Security Extensions (SMSE)

  https://h20392.www2.hp.com/portal/swdepot/displayProductInfo.do?productNumber=SecurityExt

- HP-UX Host Intrusion Detection System Version 4.1 Administrator's Guide

  http://h20000.www2.hp.com/bc/docs/support/SupportManual/c02049321/c02049321.pdf?jumpid=reg_R1002_USEN

APPENDIX

Secure Shell (SSH) is s a program used to log into another computer over a network for the purpose of executing commands on the remote machine, and perhaps to move files from one machine to another. The advantage it has over Telnet (and similarly insecure programs) is that it provides strong authentication and secure communications (encryption) over insecure channels. It is a replacement for telnet, rlogin, rsh, rcp, and rdist. Secure file transfer protocols using SSH include Secure Copy (SCP) and SSH File Transfer Protocol (SFTP).

There are two versions of SSH – SSHv1 and SSHv2. The reason for this is that a vulnerability was found in SSHv1 that allowed hackers to run code with root access. SSHv2 was created in 1995 that fixed this issue, but the fix made it impossible for SSHv1 to communicate with SSHv2.

SSHv2 provides several improvements over its predecessor:

- Support for stronger encryption ciphers, such as Triple Data Encryption Standard (3DES) and Advanced Encryption Standard (AES)

- The use of better cryptographic MAC algorithms for integrity checking

- Support for public key certificates, also known as "digital certificates"

SSHv2 is certified under the FIPS 140-1 and 140-2 NIST/U.S. government cryptographic standards. SSHv2 also replaced Trivial File Transfer Protocol (TFTP) with SFTP for file transfer (Tip: TFTP is commonly found enabled on routers and switches).

www.ingramcontent.com/pod-product-compliance
Lightning Source LLC
Chambersburg PA
CBHW021922170526

45157CB00005B/2151